Keimyung Character Education Series - 1

Global Citizenship

Global Citizenship for University Students

Workbook

Name : ______________________

Department : ______________________

Student ID : ______________________

I N T R O

–

Keimyung Global Citizenship program consists of students' experiences and activities which are distinct from regular classes and lectures.

–

The 'Keimyung Global Citizen Program' corresponds with our university's aim of education (to inspire the development of the whole person) and its objective of education (fosterage of creative specialists, ethical intellectuals, and holistic leaders). Especially, 'The Shining of the Light', the image of Keimyung, acts as a symbolic mechanism throughout the program.

–

The 'Keimyung Global Citizen Program' consists of 3 levels: myself ('Light shining on myself'), embracing others ('Light shining on others'), and then proceeding to the world ('Light shining on the world'). The majority of the program is allocated to the last stage, which matches the title of the program, 'Global Citizen'. This program is ardently supported by Keimyung University which takes pride in its distinguished international infrastructure and human resources.

–

The 'Keimyung Global Citizen Program' is designed to maximize the effectiveness of the content while minimizing the demand on students' time. In other words, the lessons from this education are stamped on the body through intimate meetings and activities. The bonds of intimacy between students and professors, and between students and students are the basis of the program. Furthermore, fostering international exchange with the nearly 1,000 foreign students who study at Keimyung University is also considered in this program's aims.

–

In Korea, there are only a few experts in character education. This program has been described in as much detail as possible to ensure that it can be conducted by novice teachers who have only basic knowledge of these concepts. It can also be used in other schools and institutions with only minimal changes to the structure.

–

The 'Keimyung Global Citizen Program' is leaving the conclusion open in order to move forward to an intensifying stage. For example, recently, there is an intensive program (Character of Christianity) based on the soul of Christianity in Keimyung University and it runs an intensive program (healing of heart) on the basis of the oriental spirit.

WHAT IS THE GLOBAL CITIZEN PROGRAM?

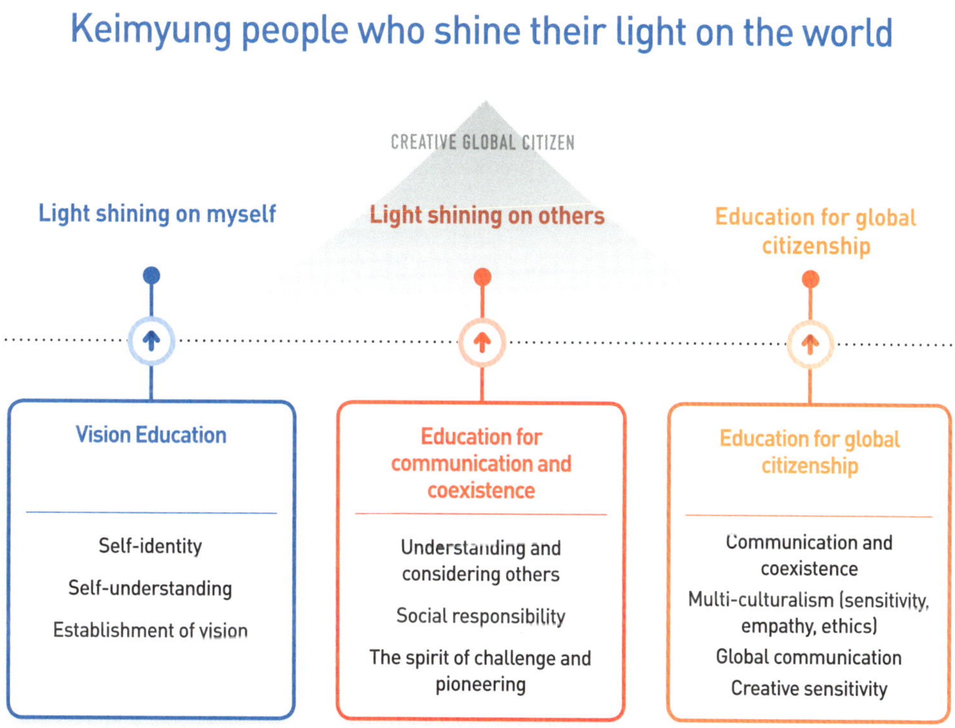

Keimyung Global Citizen Program Map

The 'Keimyung Global Citizen Program' is developed for training cultivated people of talent with upright character. The aim of this program, cultivating 'Keimyung people who shine their light on the world', is on a par with the educational aims of our university. To accomplish the goal of cultivating talented people who have expertise and good character, this program aims to compensate for the weaknesses of online courses regarding character education by pursuing character building based on activities, experiences, and practices.

Students will establish their self-identity through the Keimyung Global Citizen Program, 4 other mandatory liberal arts courses, and the 'Keimyung Spirit and Service' online course. Through these programs and classes, students will have opportunities to understand and communicate with members of society thus increasing their ability to empathize with others, and ultimately, obtain the basic virtue and knowledge required to be a global citizen.

THE CONTENTS FOR THE CURRICULUM OF EACH STAGE

STAGE	AIMS	CURRICULUM
1st stage	Light shining on myself (Vision education)	Orientation 1 (The formation of familiarity) **Describing yourself "I am ~~~~~~."**
		Vision education 1 (Self-identity formation education) **To search myself**
		Vision education 2 (Self-understanding and establishment of vision education) **The graph of my life**
2nd stage	Light shining on others (Education for communication and coexistence)	Education for communication and coexistence 1 (Understanding and considering others) **Hold my hand**
		Education for communication and coexistence 2 (Social responsibility education) **Reading and amending the Universal Declaration of Human Rights**
		Education for communication and coexistence 3 (Education for the spirit of challenge and pioneering) **Great Keimyung alumni**
3rd stage	Light shining on the world (Education for global citizenship)	Global citizenship educational practice 1 (Communication practice) **Communication through play**
		Education for global citizenship 1 (Education regarding the ethics of multi-culturalism) **Global practicum**
		Education for global citizenship 2 (Empathy Education) **Understanding others through role plays**
		Education for global citizenship 3 (Multi-cultural sensitivity education) **Making global friends**
		Practice for global citizenship 2 (Practice for cooperative problem solving) **Harmonious solution 1**
		Practice for global citizenship 3 (Cooperative problem solving presentation) **Harmonious solution 2**
		Practice for global citizenship 4 (Practice for creative sensitivity) **Painting my *Moonzado* (文子圖, calligraphy painting)**
		Education for global citizenship 4 (Education for communication and coexistence) **Searching others' treasure**
		Global citizenship education course wrap-up **Writing a review**

CONTENTS

1st Stage Vision education

1. Orientation — The formation of familiarity - **Describing yourself "I am ~~~~~~."** 08
2. Vision education 1 — Self-identity formation education - **To search myself** 12
3. Vision education 2 — Self-understanding and establishment of vision education - **The graph of my life** 20

2nd Stage Education for communication and coexistence

4. Education for communication and coexistence — Understanding and considering others - **Hold my hand** 28
5. Education for communication and coexistence 2 — Social responsibility - **Reading and amending the Universal Declaration of Human Rights** 33
6. Education for communication and coexistence 3 — Education for the spirit of challenge and pioneering - **Great Keimyung alumni** 48

3rd Stage Education for global citizenship

7. Practice for global citizenship 1 — Communication Practice - **Communication through play** 58
8. Education for global citizenship 1 — Education Regarding the Ethics of Multi-culturalism - **Global practicum** 65
9. Education for global citizenship 2 — Empathy Education - **Understanding others through role plays** 73
10. Education for global citizenship 3 — Multi-cultural Sensitivity Education - **Making global friends** 80
11. Practice for global citizenship 2 — Cooperative Problem Solving Practice - **Harmonious solution 1** 87
12. Practice for global citizenship 3 — Cooperative Problem Solving Presentation - **Harmonious solution 2** 92
13. Practice for global citizenship 4 — Practice for Creative Sensitivity - **Painting my *Moonzado* (文子圖, calligraphy painting)** 97
14. Education for global citizenship 4 — Education for Communication and Coexistence - **Searching others' treasure** 103

Global Citizenship Education Course Wrap-up - **Writing a review** 107

Light shining on myself _ Vision education for exploring my true self

step 01

Vision education

KEIMYUNG GLOBAL CITIZEN PROGRAM WORKBOOK

Light shining on myself

Vision education for exploring my true self

1. Orientation

The formation of familiarity

I am

~~~~~.

~~~~~

1. Orientation _ The formation of familiarity

Describing yourself "I am ~~~~~."

Aims

Students will be able to acknowledge the significance and necessity of character education.

-

Students will be able to recognize that character education requires a participation-based class instead of a theory-based class.

-

Students will develop hopes and expectations for character education.

-

Students will get more familiar with their classmates.

Introduction (5 minutes)

Listen to the professor's introduction.

-

Students will introduce themselves briefly.

Development (65 minutes)

Listen to the outline and the significance of the Keimyung Global Citizenship Program.

-

Listen to the curriculum and syllabus of this course.

-

Create a name tag using a special name/nickname that represents yourself. Then, on an A4 paper, explain the reason why the name was selected and memorize the other students' names.

Wrap-up (5 minutes)

The professor will help you understand the expectations of this program.

Activity materials

Write down your nickname and write the reasons why you chose that nickname.

My nickname is

____ .

Write why you chose your nickname:

____

____

____

____

____

KEIMYUNG GLOBAL CITIZEN PROGRAM WORKBOOK

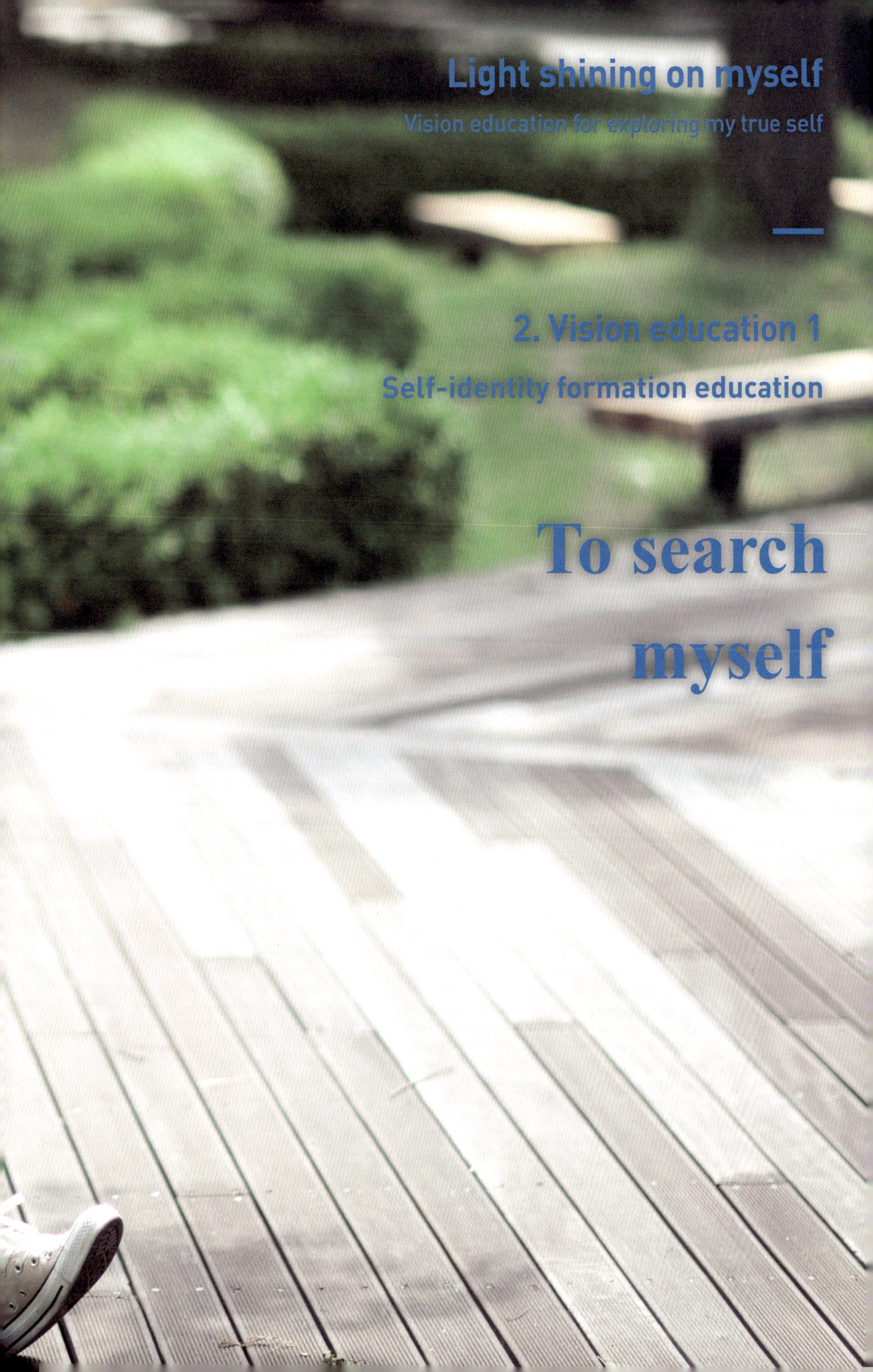

Light shining on myself

Vision education for exploring my true self

2. Vision education 1

Self-identity formation education

To search myself

2. Vision education 1 _ Self-identity formation education

To search myself

Aims

Students will be able to find an answer to who they are and to understand themselves.

–

Students will be able to meet their true self.

–

Students will be able to define and describe their self-image.

Introduction (5 minutes)

Understand the aims of the activities.

–

Meet yourself by using a cell phone camera.

Development (60 minutes)

Select one image after looking at yourself on the display screen of a cell phone (10 minutes).

–

Draw a mind map about why you chose the image (15 minutes).

–

Present the image that you chose in groups (10 minutes).

–

Share any thoughts or realizations you had in groups and then with the whole class (10 minutes).

–

Write what you want to say to yourself (15 minutes).

Wrap-up (10 minutes)

Present your thoughts regarding your self-image and reflect on the activity of exploring yourself.

Activity materials

'To search myself' is introduced as follows.

1. What is it 'to search myself'?

The aim of this program is to have an opportunity to ask yourself who you are and to search for an answer. We tend to understand ourselves based on the evaluations of us by others instead of understanding and acknowledging ourselves. Knowing, acknowledging, and loving yourself can be the foundation of life.

Through this program, you will be able to ask and answer to yourself about being aware of your preciousness, respecting your life, thinking about who you are, and loving yourself sincerely.

2. The expected effects of defining your self-image

Defining a self-image is the process of searching one's self 'to achieve the aim of finding one's self'. Through this process, you will be able to recall individuality and memory, and experience a free and comfortable atmosphere which can help to open your mind. In addition, through finding a self-image, you can think about yourself and be interested in what makes you who you are.

Ultimately, you will have an opportunity to understand and love yourself.

3. Finding my image / Saying what I want to tell myself

A lonely fighter / Were you really heart-broken at that time?

A lonely loner / I love ○○! I am here for you.♡

A lone traveller / People get you wrong! You are actually a people person…

A nerd / I am proud of you because you try your best!

A weary soul / ○○, are you tired? I will cheer you up.

Write down the image that you have chosen and make a mind map based on the reasons why you chose that image.

The image that I have chosen is

____ .

Share the images with your group and complete the chart below.

Name of group member	Keyword for image	The most impressive part	What you felt

Ask yourself who you are.

Classification	○○ is ________ to me.	The reasons why you think so
Love		
Happiness		
Friendship		
Family		
Work		
Sadness		
Wounded heart		
Memory		

Write down how you felt while participating in this session.

KEIMYUNG GLOBAL CITIZEN PROGRAM WORKBOOK

3. Vision education 2

Self-understanding and establishment of vision education

The graph of my life

3. Vision education 2 _ Self-understanding and education for vision establishment

The graph of my life

Aims

Students will be able to reflect on their life and come to accept it.

–

Students will be able to specifically picture their future life.

Introduction (15 minutes)

Recognize the aims of the activities.

–

Use a BINGO game to consider the meaning of life.

Development (45 minutes)

Recall the happiest, the saddest, the most difficult, or the most successful moment of your life (5 minutes).

–

Predict some important events in your future life (5 minutes).

–

Mark your happiest moment higher on the page and your saddest moment lower based on the reference line (see the sample) (15 minutes).

–

Present on who you were, are, and will be to your group members (20 minutes).

Wrap-up (15 minutes)

Share how you felt through creating your life graph or listening to other students' presentations.

Activity materials

Bingo Game

MY LIFE GRAPH (SAMPLE)

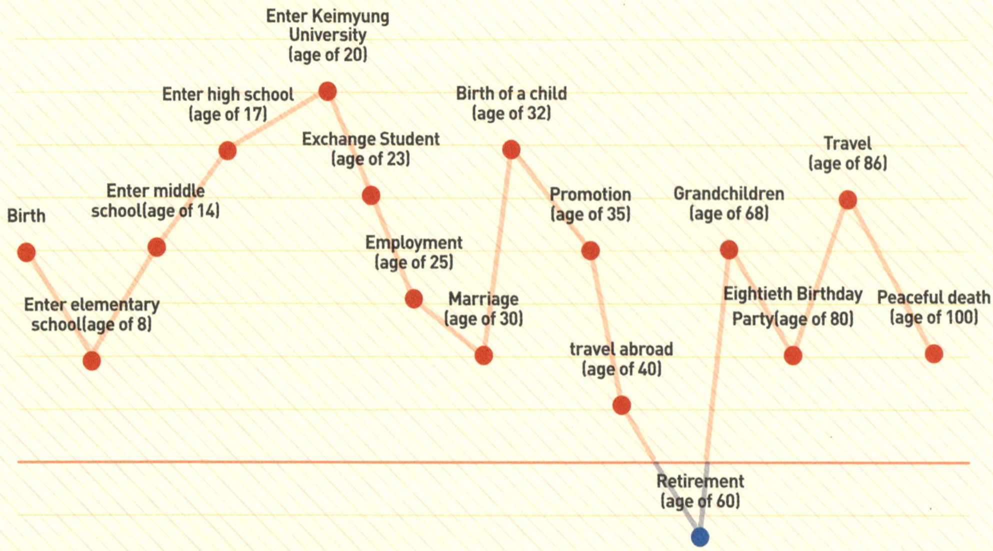

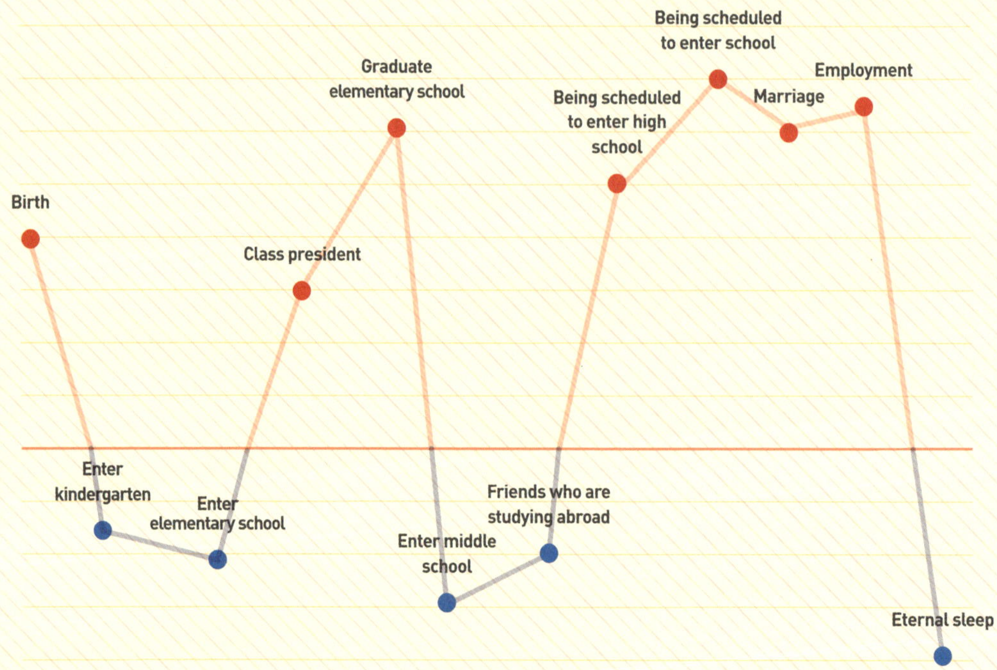

MY LIFE GRAPH

Write down how you felt while participating in this session.

step 02

Education for communication and coexistence

KEIMYUNG GLOBAL CITIZEN PROGRAM WORKBOOK

Light shining on others

Education for communication and coexistence with others

4. Education for communication and coexistence 1

Understanding and considering others

Hold my hand

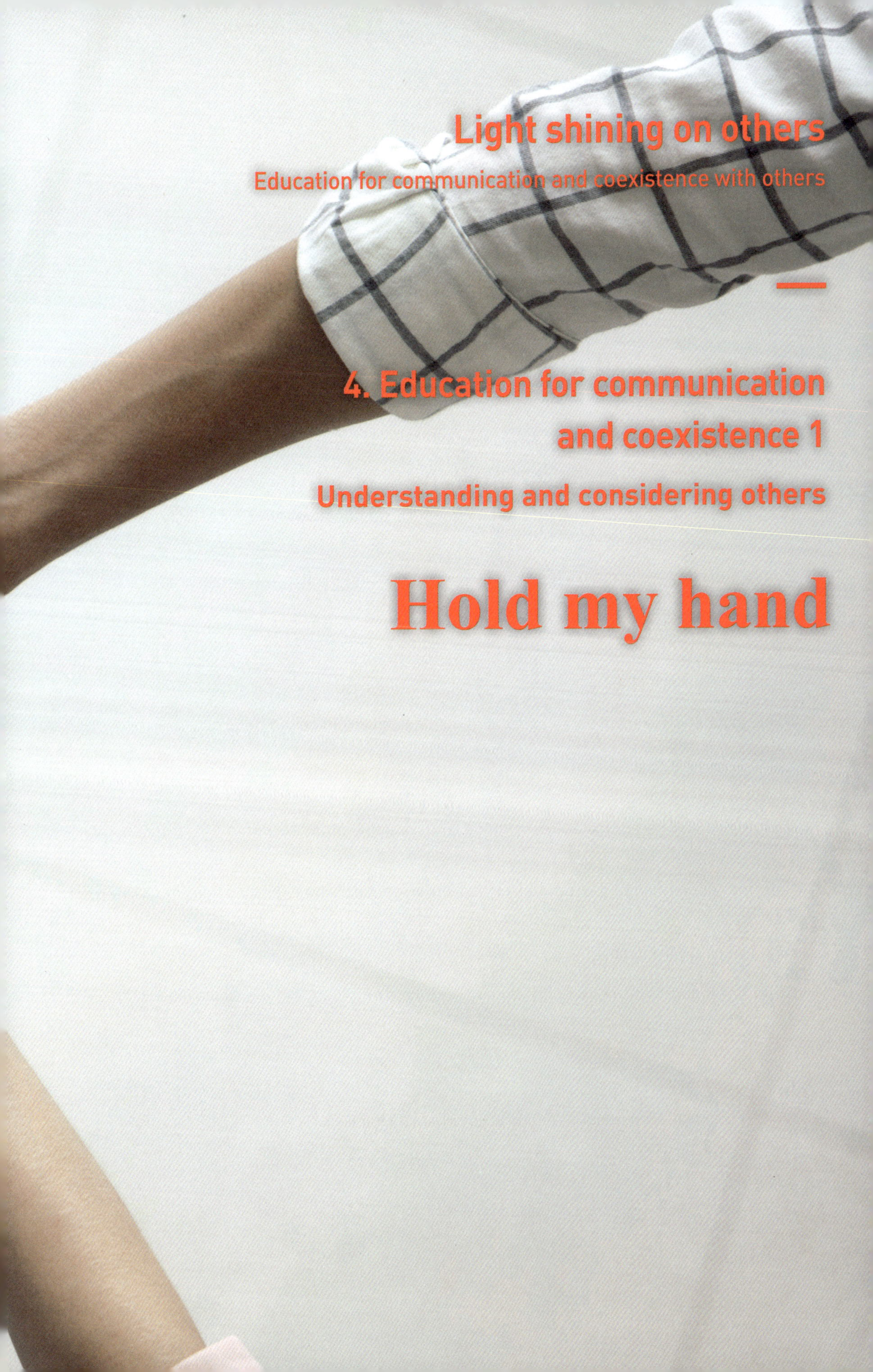

4. Education for communication and coexistence 1
_ Understanding and considering others

Hold my hand

Aims

Students will be able to establish a sense of trust in others.
–
Students will be able to think from other people's perspectives and empathize with others.
–
Students will be able to realize the true meaning of consideration.

Introduction (10 minutes)

Recognize the aims of the activities.
–
Think about some precautionary aspects of guiding visually impaired people.

Development (45 minutes)

Make pairs and select the roles of guide and visually impaired person in order to conduct the activity.
–
Help the visually impaired person to use other senses when guiding him/her (15 minutes).
–
Switch roles (15 minutes).
–
Share any thoughts or realizations you had in groups and then with the whole class (15 minutes).

Wrap-up (20 minutes)

Watch some related video clips and present what you think.

Activity materials

The list of feedback questions is presented as follows.

- What did you feel like when you acted as a visually impaired person?
- What kind of assistance did you feel was most needed when you were visually impaired?
- What did the guide do that helped you the most?
- How did you feel when you became a guide?
- What did you do well as a guide?
- What would you have liked your guide to do more of or do differently?
- Do you have any experience in assisting someone in need of help?
- How much consideration do you think we need in order to live in the world together?
- What do you think is the value of your eyes that you have not recognized so far?
- Did you feel anything new when you used your other senses?
- Do you have any prejudices against visually impaired people?
- Have you been in a situation where you had to count on someone else in your life?
- What does it mean to trust others?

Write down how you felt while participating in this session.

5. Education for communication and coexistence 2

Social responsibility

Reading and amending the Universal Declaration of Human Rights

5. Education for communication and coexistence 2
_ Social responsibility

Reading and amending the Universal Declaration of Human Rights

Aims

Students will be able to acknowledge individuality and equality.

–

Students will be able to understand human rights as equal beings.

–

Students will be able to acknowledge rules that should be observed as a global citizen.

Introduction (5 minutes)

Understand the aims of the activities.

–

Listen to an explanation about the reading and writing activities regarding the Universal Declaration of Human Rights.

Development (65 minutes)

Listen to a brief explanation about the significance and structure of the Universal Declaration of Human Rights (10 minutes).

–

Watch a video clip regarding the Universal Declaration of Human Rights (10 minutes).

–

Present the most impressive and empathetic parts of the video clip in groups (20 minutes).

–

Write what you would like to revise, complement, or add to the Universal Declaration of Human Rights on a piece of paper and display it on the board (15 minutes).

–

A representative student from each group will briefly explain their work (10 minutes).

Wrap-up (5 minutes)

Listen to each group's explanation and summarize the revised parts.

Activity materials

Read and discuss the Universal Declaration of Human Rights.

Universal Declaration of Human Rights

PREAMBLE

Whereas recognition of the inherent dignity and of the equal and inalienable rights of all members of the human family is the foundation of freedom, justice and peace in the world,

Whereas disregard and contempt for human rights have resulted in barbarous acts which have outraged the conscience of mankind, and the advent of a world in which human beings shall enjoy freedom of speech and belief and freedom from fear and want has been proclaimed as the highest aspiration of the common people,

Whereas it is essential, if man is not to be compelled to have recourse, as a last resort, to rebellion against tyranny and oppression, that human rights should be protected by the rule of law,

Whereas it is essential to promote the development of friendly relations between nations,

Whereas the peoples of the United Nations have in the Charter reaffirmed their faith in fundamental human rights, in the dignity and worth of the human person and in the equal rights of men and women and have determined to promote social progress and better standards of life in larger freedom,

Whereas Member States have pledged themselves to achieve, in cooperation with the United Nations, the promotion of universal respect for and observance of human rights and fundamental freedoms,

Whereas a common understanding of these rights and freedoms is of the greatest importance for the full realization of this pledge,

Now, therefore, The General Assembly, Proclaims this Universal Declaration of Human Rights as a common standard of achievement for all peoples and all nations, to the end that every individual and every organ of society, keeping this Declaration constantly in mind, shall strive by teaching and education to promote respect for these rights and freedoms and by progressive measures, national and international, to secure their universal and effective recognition and observance, both among the peoples of Member States themselves and among the peoples of territories under their jurisdiction.

Article 1 All human beings are born free and equal in dignity and rights. They are endowed with reason and conscience and should act towards one another in a spirit of brotherhood.

Article 2 Everyone is entitled to all the rights and freedoms set forth in this Declaration, without distinction of any kind, such as race, colour, sex, language, religion, political or other opinion, national or social origin, property, birth or other status. Furthermore, no distinction shall be made on the basis of the political, jurisdictional or international status of the country or territory to which a person belongs, whether it be independent, trust, non-self-governing or under any other limitation of sovereignty.

Article 3 Everyone has the right to life, liberty and security of person.

Article 4 No one shall be held in slavery or servitude; slavery and the slave trade shall be prohibited in all their forms.

Article 5 No one shall be subjected to torture or to cruel, inhuman or degrading treatment or punishment.

Article 6 Everyone has the right to recognition everywhere as a person before the law.

Article 7 All are equal before the law and are entitled without any discrimination to equal protection of the law. All are entitled to equal protection against any discrimination in violation of this Declaration and against any incitement to such discrimination.

Article 8 Everyone has the right to an effective remedy by the competent national tribunals for acts violating the fundamental rights granted him by the constitution or by law.

Article 9 No one shall be subjected to arbitrary arrest, detention or exile.

Article 10 Everyone is entitled in full equality to a fair and public hearing by and independent and impartial tribunal, in the determination of his rights and obligations and of any criminal charge against him.

Article 11 1. Everyone charged with a penal offence has the right to be presumed innocent until proved guilty according to law in a public trial at which he has had all the guarantees necessary for his defence.

2. No one shall be held guilty of any penal offence on account of any act or omission which did not constitute a penal offence, under national or international law, at the time when it was committed. Nor shall a heavier penalty be imposed than the one that was applicable at the time the penal offence was committed.

Article 12 No one shall be subjected to arbitrary interference with his privacy, family, home orcorrespondence, nor to attacks upon his honour and reputation. Everyone has the right to the protection of the law against such interference or attacks.

Article 13 1. Everyone has the right to freedom of movement and residence within the borders of each State.

2. Everyone has the right to leave any country, including his own, and to return to his country.

Article 14 1. Everyone has the right to seek and to enjoy in other countries asylum from persecution.

2. This right may not be invoked in the case of prosecutions genuinely arising from non-political crimes or from acts contrary to the purposes and principles of the United Nations.

Article 15 1. Everyone has the right to a nationality.

2. No one shall be arbitrarily deprived of his nationality nor denied the right to change his nationality.

Article 16 1. Men and women of full age, without any limitation due to race, nationality or religion, have the right to marry and to found a family. They are entitled to equal rights as to marriage, during marriage and at its dissolution.

2. Marriage shall be entered into only with the free and full consent of the intending spouses.

3. The family is the natural and fundamental group unit of society and is entitled to protection by society and the State.

Article 17 1. Everyone has the right to own property alone as well as in association with others.

2. No one shall be arbitrarily deprived of his property.

Article 18 Everyone has the right to freedom of thought, conscience and religion; this right includes freedom to change his religion or belief, and freedom, either alone or in community with others and in public or private, to manifest his religion or belief in teaching, practice, worship and observance.

Article 19 Everyone has the right to freedom of opinion and expression; this right includes freedom to hold opinions without interference and to seek, receive and impart information and ideas through any media and regardless of frontiers.

Article 20
1. Everyone has the right to freedom of peaceful assembly and association.
2. No one may be compelled to belong to an association.

Article 21
1. Everyone has the right to take part in the government of his country, directly or through freely chosen representatives.
2. Everyone has the right to equal access to public service in his country.
3. The will of the people shall be the basis of the authority of government; this will shall be expressed in periodic and genuine elections which shall be by universal and equal suffrage and shall be held by secret vote or by equivalent free voting procedures.

Article 22 Everyone, as a member of society, has the right to social security and is entitled to realization, through national effort and international co-operation and in accordance with the organization and resources of each State, of the economic, social and cultural rights indispensable for his dignity and the free development of his personality.

Article 23
1. Everyone has the right to work, to free choice of employment, to just and favourable conditions of work and to protection against unemployment.
2. Everyone, without any discrimination, has the right to equal pay for equal work.
3. Everyone who works has the right to just and favourable remuneration ensuring for himself and his family an existence worthy of human dignity, and supplemented, if necessary, by other means of social protection.
4. Everyone has the right to form and to join trade unions for the protection of his interests.

Article 24 Everyone has the right to rest and leisure, including reasonable limitation of working hours and periodic holidays with pay.

Article 25 1. Everyone has the right to a standard of living adequate for the health and well-being of himself and of his family, including food, clothing, housing and medical care and necessary social services, and the right to security in the event of unemployment, sickness, disability, widowhood, old age or other lack of livelihood in circumstances beyond his control.

2. Motherhood and childhood are entitled to special care and assistance. All children, whether born in or out of wedlock, shall enjoy the same social protection.

Article 26 1. Everyone has the right to education. Education shall be free, at least in the elementary and fundamental stages. Elementary education shall be compulsory. Technical and professional education shall be made generally available and higher education shall be equally accessible to all on the basis of merit.

2. Education shall be directed to the full development of the human personality and to the strengthening of respect for human rights and fundamental freedoms. It shall promote understanding, tolerance and friendship among all nations, racial or religious groups, and shall further the activities of the United Nations for the maintenance of peace.

3. Parents have a prior right to choose the kind of education that shall be given to their children.

Article 27 1. Everyone has the right freely to participate in the cultural life of the community, to enjoy the arts and to share in scientific advancement and its benefits.

2. Everyone has the right to the protection of the moral and material interests resulting from any scientific, literary or artistic production of which he is the author.

Article 28 Everyone is entitled to a social and international order in which the rights and freedoms set forth in this Declaration can be fully realized.

Article 29 1. Everyone has duties to the community in which alone the free and full development of his personality is possible.

2. In the exercise of his rights and freedoms, everyone shall be subject only to such limitations as

are determined by law solely for the purpose of securing due recognition and respect for the rights and freedoms of others and of meeting the just requirements of morality, public order and the general welfare in a democratic society.

3. These rights and freedoms may in no case be exercised contrary to the purposes and principles of the United Nations.

Article 30 Nothing in this Declaration may be interpreted as implying for any State, group or person any right to engage in any activity or to perform any act aimed at the destruction of any of the rights and freedoms set forth herein.

The overall outline of the Universal Declaration of Human Rights is as follows.

The Outline of the Universal Declaration of Human Rights

The UDHR consists of 5 parts: the preamble, the general principles of human rights, civil and political rights, the economic, social and cultural rights, and the guiding principles of human rights.

	Structure	Contents
1	Preamble	Concepts and values of human rights, goals of human rights, methods of realization of human rights, international guarantees of human rights, and obligations of member countries
2	General principles of human rights (Articles 1~2)	Freedom · equality · fraternity · anti-discrimination
3	Civil and political rights (Articles 3~21)	
4	Economic, social and cultural rights (Articles 22~27)	
5	Guiding principles on human rights (Articles 28~30)	Human rights restrictions, international relief, community duties, etc.

* The draft of the UDHR was first written in English and has later been translated into more than 350 languages.

Preamble : five paragraphs

① Whereas recognition of the inherent dignity and of the equal and inalienable rights of all members of the human family is the foundation of freedom, justice and peace in the world ⇒ concepts and values of human rights

② Whereas disregard and contempt for human rights have resulted in barbarous acts ~ it is essential to promote the development of friendly relations between nations ⇒ goals of human rights, reflection that the devastation of the Second World War resulted from ignoring human rights, 4 major human rights

③ Whereas the peoples of the United Nations have in the Charter reaffirmed their faith ~ have determined to promote social progress and better standards of life in larger freedom ⇒ methods of realization of human rights, reference of the rule of law including the right of resistance and the value of human rights

④ Whereas Member States have pledged themselves to achieve, in cooperation with the United Nations ~ is of the greatest importance for the full realization of this pledge ⇒ international guarantees of human rights

⑤ Now, therefore, the General Assembly, proclaims this Universal Declaration of Human Rights ~ both among the peoples of Member States themselves and among the peoples of territories under their jurisdiction ⇒ obligations of member countries

Article 1 – 2: general principles of human rights

Article 1: freedom, equality, fraternity
Article 2: equality and anti-discrimination

Article 3 – Article 21: civil and political rights

Article – Article 5: freedom of life and personal security (right to life, freedom from slavery, freedom from torture)
Article 6 – Article 8: protection from the law (right to recognition as a person before the law, right to equality before the law, right to remedy by competent tribunal)
Article 9 – Article 11: freedom from human bondage (freedom from arbitrary arrest and exile, right to fair public hearing, right to be considered innocent until proven guilty)
Article 12: freedom from interference with privacy
Article 13: right to free movement in and out of the country
Article 14: right to asylum in other countries from persecution
Article 15: right to a nationality and the freedom to change it
Article 16: right to marriage
Article 17: right to own property
Article 18: freedom of belief, conscience and religion
Article 19: freedom of opinion and information
Article 20: freedom of assembly and association
Article 21: right to participate in government (and in free elections)

Article 22 – Article 27: right to society, economy, and culture

Article 22: right to social security
Article 23: right to desirable work
Article 24: right to rest and leisure
Article 25: right to adequate living standard
Article 26: right to education
Article 27: right to participate in the cultural life of community

Article 28 – Article 30: guiding principles on human rights

Article 28: right to a social order that articulates this document
Article 29: community duties essential to free and full Development
Article 30: freedom from state or personal interference in the above rights

* Summarize from "'world' and 'human rights' in terms of the Universal Declaration of Human Rights" by referring to National Human Rights Commission.

Explore the terms related to human rights using a dictionary.

Below are the lexical meanings of the words related to human rights

Human rights
The basic rights to which all humans are considered to be entitled.

Prejudice
An idea or opinion formed beforehand without objective judgment or rational examination.

Discrimination
Distinction between two or more objects based on class, category, or levels.

Exclusivity
The state or quality of being exclusive. Not permitting the existence of other rights with the same content as the right to a single object.

Preconception
An opinion or conception formed in advance of adequate knowledge or experience, especially implying a negative meaning. A wrong idea formed beforehand without making a detailed judgment about any fact or person.

Write about what you found to be the most impressive or empathetic statement in the Universal Declaration of Human Rights.

Write what you would like to revise, complement, or add to the Universal Declaration of Human Rights.

Write the 5 words that you think best represent what human rights mean to you.

01

02

03

04

05

KEIMYUNG GLOBAL CITIZEN PROGRAM WORKBOOK

Light shining on others

Education for communication and coexistence with others

6. Education for communication and coexistence 3

Education for the spirit of challenge and pioneering

Great Keimyung alumni

6. Education for coexistence and communication 3 _ Education for the spirit of challenge and pioneering

Great Keimyung alumni

Aims

Students will be able to reflect on what they should abandon and keep in their life to achieve their dreams.

–

Students will be able to enhance the spirit of challenge and pioneering through the successful stories of Keimyung alumni.

–

Students will be able to reinforce their intrinsic motivation to discover the light within themselves.

Introduction (5 minutes)

Understand the aims of the activities.

–

Watch a video clip and listen to the explanation about the class activities.

Development (60 minutes)

Watch the video clip, Great Keimyung Alumni.
Think about the spirit of challenge and pioneering while watching a video of successful alumni (15 minutes).

-

Write about 'the light' that you discovered in yourself (5 minutes).

-

Draw a mind map after considering the challenge of what you should abandon and keep in your life (10 minutes).

-

Write about what you should learn from the successful Keimyung alumni in the video (10 minutes).

-

Present what you wrote (20 minutes).

Wrap-up (10 minutes)

Share any thoughts or realizations you had related to the video.

Activity materials

Write about 'the light' that you discovered in yourself.

Activity materials

Draw a mind map about what you decided to give up in order to challenge yourself.

I will abandon these for my dreams and goals!

Activity materials

Draw a mind map about what you decided to keep in order to challenge yourself.

I will keep these for
my dreams and goals!

Activity materials

Write about what you think you will learn from the successful Keimyung alumni video.

Write down how you felt while participating in this session.

step 03

Education for global citizenship

KEIMYUNG GLOBAL CITIZEN PROGRAM WORKBOOK

Light shining on the world

Education for harmonious global citizenship

7. Practice for global citizenship 1

Communication practice

Communication through play

7. Practice for global citizenship 1 _ Communication practice

Communication through play

Aims

Students will be able to increase their sense of affinity through play.

–

Students will be able to understand the functions of communication that play entails.

–

Students will be able to enhance relational and creative communication ability through play.

Introduction (15 minutes)

Introduce the aims of the activities through play.

–

Explore the effects of the play activities.

Development (45 minutes)

Explain the activities called 'communication through play' (3 minutes).

–

Encourage the students to actively participate in play activities (25 minutes).

–

Present the effects of play (17 minutes).

Wrap-up (15 minutes)

Choose a word that represents your impression of the activities, then share it with your group.

–

Summarize the effects of communication through play using the words shared by your group members.

"Communication through play" is introduced as follows.

1. What is play?

Play can express relationships in which your physical and mental aspects are coordinated and communicated in a pleasant state. Take a traditional Korean board game *'Yut'* for instance. On New Year's Day, when the game is in full swing, you shuffle *Yut* sticks and hope to cast them well so that you can get *'Yut'* or *'Mo'*, which are worth 4- and 5-space advancements respectively. Surrounded by the cheers of encouragement, you throw the sticks with firm determination to win the game. If the result is good, you will likely express the joy with both your body and mind. In this short example, you can find yourself thinking and acting on your own. Even if you get disappointed at a bad result or bicker with others about the misplaced *mals* (horses) on the board, you can still feel comforted, encouraged, or urged on by the crowd and the game continues.

Through play, you can positively activate your mental and physical aspects, discovering and experiencing ways of dealing with various situations in a relation-oriented way. As your communication ability improves, your interpersonal skills will also be enhanced and you will find opportunities to cultivate a community spirit. Play has a positive function in communication as you learn to understand various characteristics and situations regarding individuals and groups.

2. The effects of play regarding communication

People are constantly communicating with each other. Whenever and wherever you play, you can freely and naturally interact with others using various physical and mental aspects. Communication involves conscious and unconscious aspects, as well as verbal and nonverbal forms of expressions. During play, you can observe each other—listening to and watching not only verbal elements, but also nonverbal ones such as tone of voice, speed of words, gestures and movements, facial expressions, attitudes, and various behaviors—and express yourself freely and spontaneously, keeping yourself in tune with others.

In this process, both the physical and mental characteristics of the participants are exchanged freely and your communicative relationship is improved. Experiencing this kind of play can help you lose your inhibitions, defuse tension, and promote close and trusting relationships.

Voluntary and active participation in play can lead to improvements in your communication ability, interpersonal ability, intimacy, and creativity. Play can also contribute to enhancing your presence and self-identity. Furthermore, it can be a useful resource to develop flexible and effective communication and for enhancing relationships in multi-cultural situations.

Choose one member from the team with the best response and pay him/her two compliments.

A compliment ticket

I compliment ______________

on his/her __________ !

Shoot one compliment!

Shoot another compliment!

Write down how you felt while participating in this session.

KEIMYUNG GLOBAL CITIZEN PROGRAM WORKBOOK

Light shining on the world

Education for harmonious global citizenship

8. Education for global citizenship 1

Education regarding the ethics of multi-culturalism

Global practicum

8. Education for global citizenship 1
_ Education regarding the ethics of multi-culturalism

Global practicum

Aims

Students will consider methods for effective communication with foreigners in a global village and practice communicating with them.

-

Students will be able to acknowledge the multi-cultural society of Korea.

-

Students will learn about various manners from different countries and explore the differences.

-

Students will look at how to interpret body language and learn basic greetings in various languages.

Introduction (5 minutes)

Understand the aims of the activities.

-

Recognize how close the world has become as a global village.

Development (60 minutes)

Think about why Koreans have difficulty communicating in the international community and talk about the cases of 'Ugly Koreans' (5 minutes).

-

Investigate body language and etiquette common in other countries (students) and attempt to communicate in a new style (25 minutes).

-

Practice the greetings of foreign cultures (students) (20 minutes).

-

Make an interesting slogan using what was learned (10 minutes).

Wrap-up (10 minutes)

Share any thoughts or realizations you had during this session.

Activity materials

Basic etiquette

1. The essence of etiquette

1) Have an attitude of respect and understanding toward others.
2) Walk in another person's shoes: try to understand others' cultures.
3) All doors open to courtesy.
4) Fluency in a foreign language does not necessarily entail global etiquette.

2. The distinction between etiquette and manners

Etiquette refers to a norm that people should abide by, and manners refer to the way people follow the norm. For example, whether to knock or not is etiquette, whereas how to knock is manners.

3. Why global etiquette is necessary

1) The world is getting closer.
2) Korea is rapidly developing into a multi-cultural society.
3) Global citizenship is a requirement for future intellectuals.

4. The universal principle of favorability

1) Be on time.
2) Use appropriate language.
3) Have a courteous and positive attitude.
4) Be concerned.
5) Dress appropriately.
6) Be discreet.

5. Basic table manners

1) Allow ladies to sit first.
2) Unfold your napkin under the table and put it in your lap.
3) Do not gesture with a knife or fork in your hands while talking.
4) Do not speak while eating, and do not chew loudly.

What negative impressions might some Koreans create for foreigners?

The cases of ugly Koreans

1. A pamphlet published by the American Chamber of Commerce

"Koreans don't smile. Do not think they are angry by their poker face. Rather, be careful when they smile. They may smile when they want something from you or when they need to hide something."

(Source: http://cfile2.uf.tistory.com/attach/21255C435264E324175B6C)

2. 'Ugly Koreans' in the eyes of foreigners

1) don't apologize when they bump into you,

2) look angry all the time,

3) bring their own food such as kimchi to a restaurant and eat it there,

4) are sensitive to seniority based on age,

5) take things from hotels or restaurants,

6) force foreigners to sing even when they are reluctant to do so,

7) write names or draw graffiti on cultural assets,

8) speak loudly in public places,

9) approach foreigners with the purpose of practicing English,

10) have a racist attitude,

11) keep sniffling and don't blow their nose,

12) and ask for a discount.

Taboo gestures around the world

Gesture	Regions	Meaning
An embrace or physical contact	Middle East	It is forbidden to attempt to touch a woman.
Patting someone on the head	Southeast Asia	The head is deemed to contain a soul and it is best to avoid patting a child on the head.
Locking your fingers together	Some Latin American countries including Guatemala	Locking your fingers together means death.
A curled index finger in a beckoning motion	Yugoslavia, Malaysia, Vietnam, Japan, Australia	This gesture is used for animals. This gesture is used for servants or subordinates. It may mean a lewd suggestion. It may be a sign for prostitution.
A wink	Europe, USA, India, Taiwan, Australia, Nigeria	It may mean a joke. It may be considered insulting. It may be regarded as rude. It can be the vulgar behavior of bullies. It may be a sign for children to leave the room.
Stroking your chin	Korea, France, Brazil, Italy	It can be an unintentional behavior when you are lost in thought and it may mean you are bored. It may mean you have no idea. It can be like saying to someone "Beat it!".

Create a slogan for cultural etiquette around the world.

Let's learn greetings from foreign countries and practice them.

Here are some greetings from around the world

Korean	Annyeonghaseyo
USA	Hello
Japan	Konnichiwa
Italia	Buongiorno
Vietnam	Xin chào
India	Namaste
Russia	Zdravstvujtye
Germany	Guten tag
Poland	Dzień dobry
France	Bonjour
China	Ni hao
Spain	Buenos días
Greece	Kalimera
The Netherlands	Goededag
Nepal	Namaste
Rumania	Bună
Bangladesh	Salam-alaikum
Ladakh in Northern India	Jullay
Brazil	Olá
Sweden	Hejsan
Kenya, Tanzania	Habari gani
Arab	As-Salam Alaikum
Haiti	Bonjou
Australia	Good day
Israel	Shalom
Indonesia	Selamat pagi
Colombia	Hola
Thailand	Sawasdee Krab [Ka for females]
Turkey	Günaydın, Merhaba
Pakistan	As-Salam-u-Alaikum
Hawaii	Aloha
Hungary	Jo napot

Write down how you felt while participating in this session.

Light shining on the world

Education for harmonious global citizenship

9. Education for global citizenship 2

Empathy Education

Understanding others through role plays

9. Education for global citizenship 2 _ Empathy Education

Understanding others through role plays

Aims

Students will come to understand the ethos of multi-culturalism.

-

Students will be able to cultivate their character as a global citizen.

-

Students will be able to understand the role of foreigner as a social minority.

Introduction (5 minutes)

Understand the aims of the activities.

-

Understand the format of the role plays.

Development (60 minutes)

Choose a theme and make a plot for a story.

-

Ensure that every member of the group participates in the role play (35 minutes).

-

Perform the role plays in front of the class for 5 minutes (25 minutes).

Wrap-up (10 minutes)

Share your thoughts and realizations from planning and making the role plays.

-

Present what you felt about the activity.

Activity materials

The role play is as follows.

1. What is a role play?

A role play refers to indirectly experiencing a situation that we have not been exposed to or to playing the role of another person. Through a role play, we can gain new insights into our own and others' behaviors. By acting out an adopted role, we get an opportunity to analyze and assess our own attitudes and behaviors. This is a meaningful tool that can help us recognize problems and gives us opportunities to find solutions to them.

2. Expected effects of a role play

Role plays provide participants with an opportunity to identify their personality and talents and to experience a sense of community and pleasure from participating in the process. It also enables participants to understand and appreciate the meaning of their roles and to have confidence in the accomplishments through the opportunity to present them in front of others.

3. The themes of role plays for the education of global citizenship

- If a Pakistani friend has lost his wallet on the bus and asks for your help
- If you meet an immigration officer who is exceptionally demanding of people of color when you go through the US immigration process
- If your friend is bullied just because his mother is Vietnamese
- If you talk to a French friend about Koreans eating dog meat
- If your parents object to your marrying a foreign girlfriend
- If your friend wants to break up with you because of your different religion
- If an immigration officer treats your Chinese friend studying here like an illegal immigrant
- If an American woman gives birth to a child and then wants to take a shower and go out the next day
- If you have to use one row of toilets with no doors in China
- If a Westerner sees Koreans eating a stew in a pot together without using an individual bowl

Create a plot for a role play.

Considering the plot for the role play, create some characters and write a script to complete the role play.

Character	Role player	Role player's lines

Write down how you felt while watching the role plays.

Group name	Theme	The most impressive part	Any disappointing parts	The best role player	Something you learned

Write down how you felt while participating in this session.

KEIMYUNG
GLOBAL CITIZEN
PROGRAM
WORKBOOK

Light shining on the world

Education for harmonious global citizenship

10. Education for global citizenship 3

Multi-cultural sensitivity education

Making global friends

10. Education for global citizenship 3
_ Multi-cultural sensitivity education

Making global friends

Aims

Students will listen to an explanation about how globalized Korean society has become.

-

Students will get to know some foreign students at KMU.

-

Students will try to extend care and consideration to foreigners staying in Korea.

Introduction (5 minutes)

Listen to the aims of the activities.

-

Listen to some reasons why the foreign students were invited to be assistants and listen to the students' introductions.

Development (60 minutes)

Learn about the status of some of the foreign students studying at KMU (10 minutes).

-

Listen to stories from the foreign students about their experiences and feelings regarding Korea and KMU (20 minutes).

-

Have interview style conversations with the foreign students in groups (25 minutes).

-

Briefly write your impressions of meeting the foreign students (5 minutes).

Wrap-up (10 minutes)

Present your feelings regarding the session and then share them with each other.

Notice

The instructor should get the information on the foreign students working as assistants in advance.

-

The instructor should check the presentation time of the foreign students beforehand lest it should be too long.

Activity materials

The status of the foreign students studying at KMU (2nd semester, 2016)

Oct. 1st, 2016 / enrolled students

Nation	Doctoral program	Master's program	Bachelor's program	Total
Ghana	0	1	0	1
Nigeria	0	1	1	2
Nepal	0	1	0	1
Taiwan	0	0	3	3
Germany	0	0	1	1
Russia	0	0	1	1
Mexico	0	1	1	2
Mongolia	0	15	5	20
USA	1	3	3	7
Bangladesh	1	0	0	1
Vietnam	0	7	19	26
Brazil	0	0	1	1
Saudi Arabia	0	2	11	13
Sri Lanka	0	1	9	10
Angola	0	0	2	2
UK	0	0	1	1
Uzbekistan	3	29	9	41

Nation	Doctoral program	Master's program	Bachelor's program	Total
India	0	0	1	1
Indonesia	0	3	4	7
Japan	0	1	3	4
China	10	70	541	621
Chile	0	1	0	1
Cameroon	0	2	0	2
Kazakhstan	0	3	0	3
Cambodia	0	4	2	6
Canada	1	0	1	2
Tajikistan	0	4	4	8
Tanzania	0	0	1	1
Thailand	0	1	0	1
Turkmenistan	0	1	0	1
Pakistan	0	3	0	3
The Philippines	1	3	2	6
Total	**17**	**157**	**626**	**800**

Write down your thoughts about the foreign students in KMU as well as other foreigners you have met.

Positive images :

Negative images :

Make interview questions about living in Korea as a foreign student.

Questions	Answers	Opinions on the answers

Write down how you felt while participating in this session.

11. Practice for global citizenship 2

Cooperative problem solving practice

Harmonious solution 1

11. Practice for global citizenship 2
_ Cooperative problem solving practice

Harmonious solution 1

Aims

Students will strengthen mutual bonds with foreign students.

-

Students will learn about some global issues through others' perspectives and discuss solutions to them.

-

Students will learn to cooperate with others to pursue a harmonious life.

Introduction (5 minutes)

Understand the aims of the activities.

-

Listen to an explanation of a cooperative project involving the foreign students.

Development (65 minutes)

Listen to the instructor's brief explanation of a global issue chosen as a class topic and suggest other issues (10 minutes).

-

Watch the images and video clips along with an explanation regarding "Harmonious solutions" (10 minutes).

-

Select a topic and work to find a solution to it by rewriting the lyrics of a song chosen in groups (40 minutes).

-

Arrange the rewritten lyrics of the song (5 minutes).

Wrap-up (5 minutes)

Each group will present its song in the next session.

-

Listen to the preparation regarding the presentation.

Activity materials

A "harmonious solution" is as follows.

1. What is a 'harmony solution'?

The purpose of this program is to have an opportunity to consider global issues together and find possible solutions. In this program, students recognize that the various problems that the world is facing are our problems, and they will look for various methods and solutions to settle them by gathering ideas together with the theme of peaceful coexistence. Students will rewrite the lyrics of a familiar song and sing it together in groups, considering the values of coexistence and harmony.

2. Expected effects of rewriting lyrics and singing together

Rewriting lyrics and singing together is a process and outcome for students to search for solutions to the global issues selected by each group in order to find a 'harmonious solution.' Through this process students will realize that solving global issues is a shared duty to achieve peaceful coexistence. In addition, both the ability to communicate with others, and critical and creative thinking skills can be improved in the course of exchanging diverse ideas for problem solving. Above all, through the process of singing together, students will be able to aim for a harmonious life and understand its value.

3. Several fragments of thought for peaceful coexistence

1) How to overcome religious and cultural gaps

All ideological extremisms, religious enthusiasms, and ethnocentrisms are sensitive and serious ideologies that can provoke violence and war. In order to overcome conflicts stemming from religious and cultural gaps, we should have an open attitude toward other religions and cultures. We can take this open attitude by honestly admitting that our thoughts and views are imperfect and limited, and by still striving to maintain an open mind toward others. When we realize that religious and the cultural differences give us diversity and enrich the world we live in, we will be able to overcome narrow-mindedness, self-righteousness, and dogmatism.

2) How to reduce the gap between the rich and the poor

In order to reduce the disparity between the rich and the poor, it is necessary to focus on securing tax equality between wage workers and self-employed people, solving the problem of imposing insurance premiums on the insured which is a long standing problem with social insurance, and restraining real estate speculation that deepens asset inequality. In addition, income security, self-support aid, and welfare service provisions for the low-income class and vulnerable social groups should be promoted. Above all, the government itself should have a firm will to settle the problems of poverty and discrimination. Since development and distribution are not matters of choice but are matters of harmony, nothing is more important than committing continuous concern and effort to settle them.

3) How to recover nature

There was a time when humans were proud of destroying nature and exercising control over it for their happiness and convenience. The first step to recover nature is to stop the violence toward and exploitation of it and look back on the attitude of human beings toward nature. Without asking the earnest question of what is the desired relationship between humans and nature, we cannot recover nature. Nature is not a storage of natural resources for humans, nor does it exist to offer a habitat for humans. Rather, nature has its own purpose within itself, and humans have a responsibility to help it construe its purpose.

4) Some examples of 'harmonious solutions' that can be used to create a song.

· Overcoming religious and cultural gaps
· Reducing the gap between the rich and the poor
· Recovering nature
· Making a peaceful world without war
· Making a world without discrimination
· Making a happy life

In groups, write down lyrics about the chosen global issue and its solution(s).

Global issue	
Rewritten title	
Original title	
Contents of rewritten lyrics	

KEIMYUNG GLOBAL CITIZEN PROGRAM WORKBOOK

Light shining on the world

Education for harmonious global citizenship

12. Practice for global citizenship 3

Cooperative problem solving presentation

Harmonious solution 2

12. Practice for global citizenship 3
_ Cooperative problem solving presentation

Harmonious solution 2

Aims

Students will strengthen mutual bonds with foreign students.

–

Students will learn about some global issues through others' perspectives and discuss some solutions to them

–

Students will learn to cooperate with others and pursue a harmonious life.

Introduction (5 minutes)

Understand the aims of the activities.

–

Listen to an explanation of a cooperative project involving the foreign students.

Development (65 minutes)

Decide the presentation order (5 minutes).

–

Describe the global issue that you discussed and the rewritten lyrics. Then, sing your song in groups (40 minutes).

–

Sing the songs which received the best response together (10 minutes).

Wrap-up (15 minutes)

Speak together about how you felt during the activity of seeking a solution to a global issue with songs.

Activity materials

Take notes on the global issues and the rewritten lyrics covered by the other groups.

Groups	Global issues	Rewritten lyrics

Write down how you felt while participating in this session.

13. Practice for global citizenship 4

Practice for creative sensitivity

Painting my *Moonzado* (文子圖, calligraphy painting)

13. Practice for global citizenship 4_ Practice for creative sensitivity

Painting my *Moonzado* (文字圖, calligraphy painting)

Aims

Students will build a foundation for cultural tolerance by understanding their own traditional culture.

–

Students will enhance their creativity and imagination through painting their own *Moonzado*.

–

Students will reaffirm the virtues and visions that they require.

Introduction (5 minutes)

Understand the aims of the activities.

–

Listen to an explanation of the process of painting a *Moonzado*.

Development (60 minutes)

Listen to an explanation with ppt materials regarding *Minhwa* (folk painting) and *Moonzado* (calligraphy painting) in the late Chosun Dynasty (10 minutes).

–

Select your '*Moonza* (Chinese characters)': select the Chinese characters which represent your virtues and goals (5 minutes).

–

Draw an image of your '*Moonza*': draw a *Moonzado* to express the key words of your virtues and visions (25 minutes).

–

Explain your *Moonzado* (20 minutes).

Wrap-up (10 minutes)

Present how you felt throughout the activities of selecting your *Moonza* and painting it.

Activity materials

The contents of *Minhwa* (民話) and *Moonzado* (文字圖) in the late Chosun Dynasty are as follows.

***Minhwa* and *Moonzado* in the late Chosun Dynasty**

1. *Minhwa* in the late Chosun Dynasty.

Minhwa, known as a style of folk paintings, contains underlying aesthetics and emotions of the Korean culture. Though there were strong plebeian tastes and emotions in this style, *Minhwa* was loved by the noblemen and the court, and is still considered a popular traditional culture. In that sense, *Minhwa* is one of the most representative styles of Korean painting. The genres and themes covered by *Minhwa* include "*Hawjoedo*" (painting of flowers and animals), figure painting (painting of old stories, customs and religions), several kinds of calligraphy painting, landscape painting, "*Moonbanghwa*," (still-life painting including *Chaeckgado* and *Moonbangdo* drawing books and stationeries), and "*Nugackhwa*," (painting of buildings). The paintings of peony flowers, which symbolizes a prosperous life, were hung in women's rooms, and the paintings of fish symbolizing success were hung in men's rooms in most cases; carp, catfish, and mandarin fish have the meaning of one's hope of being appointed as a public official.

2. *Moonzado* in the late Chosun Dynasty

From ancient times, Chinese characters were considered to have an infinite energy from nature and the universe. Thus, to those who could not read them, the characters were the object of a mysterious and magical power.[1] The Chinese characters contain symbolic meanings that express things or phenomena, and were originally of strong visual formality, which is sufficient enough for them to be considered a graphic design. *Moonzado* is a calligraphy painting of Chinese characters in which old stories or fables from the ancient times corresponding to the meaning of the characters are depicted in the specific parts of the characters. This style has become popular in the cultural areas that use Chinese characters including Vietnam and Japan as well as China and Korea. In the late Chosun Dynasty, various styles of *Moonzado* along with *Minhwa* became widely popular. The popularity seems to stem from national efforts to strengthen Confucian virtues and from folk religious customs of the people who suffered from various natural disasters and infectious diseases and tried to rely on the perceived power of the Chinese characters. *Moonzado*, a kind of *Minhwa*, can be

---

1) Lee, Myung Ku, *Oriental Typography, Moonzado*, Seoul: Leedia, 2005, p. 23.

classified into three types according to its theme.

1. *Byuksamoonzado* (辟邪文字圖): calligraphy paintings with a symbol of dispelling vicious ghosts such as: 龍 (dragon), 虎 (tiger), etc.

2. *Gilsangmoonzado* (吉相文字圖): calligraphy paintings with a meaning of a lucky omen like: 壽(long life), 福 (luck), 康 (comfort), 寧 (comfort), 貞 (rightness), 富(richness), 貴(nobleness)

3. *Hyozemoonzado* (孝悌文字圖): calligraphy paintings representing the 8 virtues of Confucianism, which are: 孝 (filial piety), 悌 (politeness), 忠 (loyalty), 信 (belief), 禮 (courtesy), 義 (righteousness), 廉 (integrity), 恥(shame)恥[2)]

3. *Hyozemoonzado*, the character education poster from the late Chosun Dynasty

Hyozemoonzado, also known as 'Confucian *Moonzado*', was shaped around the 18th century, and became explosively popular around the 19th century. The 8 characters of the *Hyozemoonzado* imply the 8 virtues which represent Korean traditional ethics and morals, and were also a focus of the people in the late Chosun Dynasty whose social consciousness quickly grew. Especially, as social discipline began to break down in the 18th century due to the collapse of the caste system, drunkenness, entertainment, and luxurious trends, it was decorated with enlightening and instrumental contents in order to encourage a Confucian lifestyle as the national governing ideology. A number of *Hyozemonzado* were produced using the woodcutting technique, which made them very distinct from the other kinds of *Minhwa*. As a result, it seems to have been effective as a sort of a poster for public character education in the late Chosun Dynasty.

Since it had unique designs when compared with other calligraphy paintings from other countries, and had various forms in each province, it had unique characteristics which have not been seen in other Chinese character cultures. Therefore, *Hyozemoonzado* is considered to be made well enough to compare with authentic paintings, and its esthetic is formal enough to be included in the field of graphic design today.

<*Hyozemoonzado*> in the Hengso Museum collection at Keimyung University

---

2) Lee, Myung Ku, Same Book, p. 35.

Select a character that represents a virtue or the goal you want to have, and draw a sketch for your *Moonzado*.

Write down how you felt while participating in this session.

14. Education for global citizenship 4

Education for communication and coexistence

Searching others' treasures

14. Education for global citizenship 4
_ Education for communication and coexistence

Searching others' treasures

Aims

Students will re-establish their identity by finding their personal merits through the eyes of others.

-

Students will change the ways of understanding others by looking at other people's merits instead of their faults.

-

Students will overcome inferiority and helplessness, and establish positive human relations.

Introduction (5 minutes)

Understand the aims of the activities.

-

Understand the meaning of the activities.

Development (50 minutes)

Each student writes down his or her name on an activity sheet, and all of the sheets are circulated to the group members.

-

Group members write down specific merits of the person whose name is written on the activity sheet (20 minutes).

-

The group is given time to listen to your merits as told by other group members (30 minutes).

Wrap-up (5 minutes)

Write down your impressions of the activity.

-

Listen to the closing remarks of the program.

Activity materials

Let's make a list for a treasure hunt to search for the merits of others.

Searching ___________'s treasure

What is this person's treasure? When and how was the treasure discovered? Why is it a treasure? How will the treasure affect this person in a positive way in the future?

Treasure (Merit)	Specific behavior or situation	Future vision	Name

Write how you felt while participating in the treasure hunt.

Keimyung Global citizenship education course wrap-up _ Writing a review

Aims

Students will be able to understand the meaning of Keimyung Global Citizenship.

-

Students will be able to acknowledge their role as a global citizen.

Introduction (3 minutes)

Have an overview of the Keimyung global citizenship program, and review the goals of the each session.

Development (9 minutes)

Write down briefly how you felt, what you realized, and how you changed while participating in this program (6 minutes).

-

Present and share what you wrote with your group members (3 minutes).

Wrap-up (3 minutes)

Identify your roles as a Keimyung Global Citizen and complete the program.

Write down how you felt, what you learned, and how you changed while participating in the Keimyung Global Citizen program.

Global Citizenship for University Students

Authors

Cho, Myeong Sil (Tabula Rasa College, Keimyung University)
-
Hur, Seon Ho (Tabula Rasa College, Keimyung University)
-
Kim, Hyang Sook (Tabula Rasa College, Keimyung University)
-
Kim, Jae Hyun (Tabula Rasa College, Keimyung University)
-
Kim, Kyung Mi(Tabula Rasa College, Keimyung University)
-
Lee, Hyun Ji (Tabula Rasa College, Keimyung University)
-
Lee, Kyung Kyu (Tabula Rasa College, Keimyung University)

Translators

Kim, Woo Hyung (Tabula Rasa College, Keimyung University)
-
Kim, Young Hee (Tabula Rasa College, Keimyung University)
-
Sohn, Na Gyung (Tabula Rasa College, Keimyung University)

Editor

Kerr, Robert Charles (Tabula Rasa College, Keimyung University)

Global Citizenship for University Students

First printing	Feb. 22, 2017
First edition publication	Feb. 28, 2017
Authors	Global Citizenship Textbook Compilation Committee
Translators	Kim Woo Hyung, Kim Young Hee, Sohn Na Gyung
Executive director of publishing	Synn Ilhi
Publisher	Keimyung University Press
	registration 347-1998-1 (Sep. 1st, 1970)
Address	Keimyung University, 1095 Dalgubeol-daero, Dalseo-Gu, Daegu 42601, Korea
Phone	053-580-6233
Fax	053-580-6235
Homepage	www.kmupress.com

ISBN 978-89-7585-771-3 03320 Price ₩5,000

The cataloging in publication (CIP) of this book is available in the web-sites of Bibliographic Information and Distribution Support System(http://seoji.nl.go.kr) and Korean Library Information System(http://www.nl.go.kr/kolisnet). (CIP control number: CIP2017005111)